OTHER WORKS BY JOHN W. SEXTON

POETRY

The Prince's Brief Career (Cairn Mountain Press, 1996)
Shadows Bloom / Scáthanna Faoi Bhláth (Doghouse, 2004)
Vortex (Doghouse, 2005)
Petit Mal (Revival Press, 2009)

NOVELS FOR CHILDREN

The Johnny Coffin Diaries (The O'Brien Press, 2001)
Johnny Coffin School-Dazed (The O'Brien Press, 2002)

CD

Sons of Shiva (Track Records, 2003)

RADIO

The Ivory Tower (RTE Radio 1, 1999 – 2002)

The Offspring
of the Moon

JOHN W. SEXTON

salmonpoetry

Published in 2013 by
Salmon Poetry
Cliffs of Moher, County Clare, Ireland
Website: www.salmonpoetry.com
Email: info@salmonpoetry.com

Copyright © John W. Sexton, 2013

ISBN 978-1-908836-28-1

COVER ARTWORK: © *Ludmila Korol. "Moon Wind", 2001,*
Oil on Canvas by Ludmila Korol – www.ludmilakorol.com
COVER DESIGN & TYPESETTING: *Siobhán Hutson*

Printed in Ireland by Sprint Print

Salmon Poetry gratefully acknowledges the support of The Arts Council

For

HARLAN JAY ELLISON

Whose fiction was my first mentor in the lyricality of imagination

Each thorn, Tom Pin,
a pointed step
up the briar staircase

Acknowledgements

Many of the poems in this collection have previously appeared in the following journals:

Poetry Ireland Review, *Poetry Chaikhana*, *Revival*, *Riddle Fence*, *Southword*, *The Stinging Fly*, *The Stony Thursday Book*, *The Tuosist Parish Newsletter*, *World Haiku Review*.

Some also appeared in the following anthologies:

Census 2 (edited by Sarah Lundberg), *The Doghouse Book of Ballad Poems* (edited by Noel King and Peter Keane), *Real Imaginings* (edited by Tommy Frank O'Connor), *Sixty Poems for Haiti* (edited by Ian Dieffenthaller and Maggie Harris), *Something Beginning With P* (edited by Seamus Cashman), *Times New Roman* (edited by Todd Swift).

Contents

Daddy-Long-Legs

We're those lopsided puppets awkward
in motion through the air. Our wings
are fractured windows of pale glass looking
out, looking in, to nothing. Our hinged
and fragile stilts still work long after
we've miscarried them. You'll see them
kicking in a young child's hair. You call us
Ghost Needles. See us hovering over
the threshold of the porch. We're the tailors
of the clothes you wear in your dreams,
the ones that fade on you the very moment
that morning's light breaches the join
in the curtain. In the damaged rigging
of spiders' webs we are discarded part,
spent fuselage; the subtle remains of night.
Then we rise again from the slumbering
grass, linger lazily at your door, silently
awaiting entry. We carry the dusk of autumn.

Inventor, 1899 - 1985

Biro, immortal in every biro,
dreams from a scribble in the margin, sulks
in grills of hatch marks, the change-of-mind o
in a noughts and crosses game; unkempt, skulks
in the bodies of a stick family,
his mind a lopsided house, its windows
curtained with scrawl. He's also the starry
sky, the stars, the moon, every ebb and flow
in the shopping list: toilet rolls, razors,
bleach, custard powder, milk, cat food, pencils.
Hungarian; four-thousand-eight-hundred-
and-sixty-eighth entry in my diction-
ary; dead; immortal in every pen;
full, dried-up, re-filled again and again.

William Blake Sees the Head Lice in Spectres

Wisps of hair weave in a braid, tangling
the teeth of his comb; grey dandruff grains dot
the deposits of grease left on the prongs.
Blake sees light as deposits too, rising
after his quiff is done, an aura's clot
coalescing, blur of brightness that sings.
It sings its name, but he cannot discern
what is said, like the Our Father backwards,
abacus knots of number on a string,
a language unknown to him, without words
he's ever heard. Then thought speaks through his hair
and he knows this is the Ghost of a Flea.
Blake has a beard growing out of each ear;
with a tuning fork he grooms eccentricity.

Soft Furnishings

Uncle Balthazar keeps his cats hidden
from the Cat Inspector. "It's obvious
from the pattern in this carpet, you're a
cat person." Uncle Balthazar coughs whoops
in protest: "Only in carpets, curtains,
and similar soft furnishings, sir. Cats
in real life make me hack up my guts; I'm
allergic, quite allergic. Their fine hairs
travel straight up the nose-pipe, kill me dead."
And he coughs again, just at the thought.
The Cat Inspector leaves and Uncle Bal
rubs the carpet with his toe, and the cat
patterns raise themselves from the pile, become
his thirteen cats, each evasive of tax.

Frog

Peeled free of my body and unfolded
over the hillside, my skin would cover
three acres, for I am the shining grass
of morning, compressed in a croaking
knot. The river I swim through is merely
the dream of the red slimy river of my gut.
I hold the world inside my mouth, ribbeting
to get out. My throat chokes the world back
to its place. I am the slippery jewel that god
coughed up when time began. I'm the soft
cog of the flesh-clock, the green spring for
winding the universe down in. In the heron's
beak I am the Omega of swallowed things.

Sunlight

I rest on top of things, but am never
at rest. On the surface of lakes, the sea, even
the tepid water in a bucket, I am restless,
flittering about, always shifting. That's the way
I am when you look me in the face, anytime
you can bear to look. I've come a long way
and can never really stop, am travelling further
yet. Wives lie out on their lawns, relishing my
touch, while their husbands stew in their own
sweat. Only women know the secret of me: to
lie perfectly still and let me accumulate on their
skin. And all those wives are mine, all of them
sitting out patiently soaking me in, none of them
jealous that I have them all, darkening under me.

In and Out of Their Heads

After he had proved irrefutably
that angels don't live on the heads of pins
or in the green cities of verdigris
that he scraped from the mute faces of coins,

Professor Lightshade discovered yeast-men,
frothing in the head with the minds of gods,
inhabiting the flat circular pen
commonly known as a ladybird's spot.

Inebriated for eternity,
smashed on fumes from their own fermenting brains,
ferried from bush to bush and tree to tree,
drunken passengers of the insect trains

the yeast-men exist devoid of futures,
travel no further than their own stupors.

Uncle Snake's Endless Tales

When he speaks, lying Uncle Snake whistles
through his tongue. This is tall-tale number six.
"A meadow-hag enchanted the thistles
and sent them to battle the local witch:

armies of furry hats on soft green sticks.
Squashing sausages with a rolling pin
the witch summoned sixty-six flattened pigs
and then worm-holed them through the garbage bin.

In seconds putrid rotting pigs as thin
as books were snuffling the meadow-hag's skirts
and drew down clouds of flies as black as sin.
The witch cackled, preening her nails and warts."

Then Uncle Snake just laughs and laughs and laughs.
"Next I'll tell you of the flying giraffes."

Pulls

The spawn of snags that laid no eggs
but waited in untended points or nails,
teased secretly the threads of sweaters,
scarves, knitted hands, drawing loose worms
of wool. Catch us by the heads and we'll
bring the bound world out with our tails.
Best not to nip us at the root, or else we'll
hole ourselves whole. Instead, force our fronts
through seamstresses' eyes and send us back
down through our own ends. Left unattended
we'll lengthen in time and unravel our own
beginnings. The stuff of accident we wait
to happen until that moment when we do.
So when you see us hanging from your clothes
know we were meant to be, for we're the in
that's supposed to be out and out we'll come.

Only One Owner, Immaculately Kept

Lord Earthheart steps towards his car
its body shining like a lacquered nail

the seats are mummified salesmen
their heads turned to face the curb

ghosts of songbirds steam
from the reconditioned engine

a tragic-warden has left a parting-ticket
behind the wind-scream wiper

the tyres are kept suitably flat
for this car that goes nowhere

Troubled Sleep

In a walled, dense garden of the city
a nightingale's song penetrated the dreams
and sleep, night after night, of those who slept,
row after row in their boxes of homes:
solicitors and clerks, secretaries,
all packed quite neatly in the trays and files
of their own sleeping heads. Dark cats waited
in the shadows, the same shadows that stirred
in the dense, garbled dreams of the dreaming.
"I am free, for now," sang the bird, awake.

She Combed the Night

she combed the night into her hair
the stars fell on her dress
she danced around him seven times
the seventh time was best

the seventh time he heard the moon
whisper its seven sins
the seven times it loved the sea
and gave her silver rings

she danced the garden paths once more
and circled seven times
he offered up his heart to her
and courted her with rhymes

he held her close and kissed her hair
the stars stuck to his face
his skin turned black as night itself
the heavens were his place

The Unintentional Portents
of Wang-Yu-Feng

Wang-Yu-Feng breaks an egg against his head
and a yellow dragon runs through his hair.
Dazed, the magician topples from his chair
as a grey heron the colour of lead
rises from his face; three tail-feathers shed
and drift towards the splintered wooden floor.
Wang-Yu-Feng's tongue suddenly tastes sour
and all his thoughts evaporate, seem bled
by some malign force. The trick with the egg
has misfired; intended only to hatch
a yolk-stained duckling that would please a child.
The Empress gasps, the heron takes her wig;
a dragon behind her loosens the catch
of her dress. One bad egg, an Empire spoiled.

Breakfast with Aladdin

With a tarnished spoon he opened a door
in the top of an egg. Comatose in
the golden slop of its own molten dream
lay the sun; radiation had jellied
into a white elliptical aura.
The door snapped on its thin hinge, came away
with a dib of the sol. Djinns erupted
on his tongue, offered three wishes apiece
for a taste of stars. "No, no, no, no, no,"
he said and banged his spoon. "I am the god
who opened the room; I am the one with
the tarnished key, that can open the door
to Eternity. It is me, it is
me, it is me. I am the Djinn, not thee."

The Ghosts of Withered Roses Haunt the Vase

As the snail withdraws its body of phlegm
from the drenched air, catkins slowly emerge
as soft fur, though formed from the same
liquid pus. We are all water, I once read,
but bound in. One with the plankton
frothing in combers, that's left to stain
the pier stones with green scum.
                              The Spirit
of Snails trembles before me, monstrous,
glowing in transparent power: beckons me
to pus and water, its dark eternities.
Outside, the garden is crushed with rain,
leaves and grasses become leached of all
their colour. Now called to water's substance,
I also begin to wane.

A Matching Coat for Her Man

With each step her bare feet
un-silvered the dewy grass.
The blossoming furze, buds
tipped with rust, unwound
in bursts of birdsong. With
a long pointed twig she gathered
a skein of spider's silk, dismantling
web after web onto her stick.

Under the flickering dust-light
of moths, her shadow seated
beside her, she made a coat
from the gathered strands. Made
a coat for her one true man, one
he could wear for the fog, stepping
visibly invisible as smoke, one
that would be lit by the sun.

Or, lit by the moon, one he could
wear to be bright as the stars, one
he could wear stepping out
with the hares; light as the air
he'd take her hand, and down
by the long lane they would walk,
their long grey coats a-stuck,
moth-light bleeding around them.

If Any

after Eugenio Montale

If any have confused you with the fox,
it will be due to that magnificent jump -
for the flying in your step joins as much
as separates, it agitates each lump
of grit in the stony path, (your terrace,
the streets near the Cottolengo, meadow,
the birch tree that quivers at the mere trace
of me, happy, humble, rotted hollow) –
or perhaps only for the luminous
wave that oscillates from your almond eyes,
for the shrewdness of your feigned surprise,
for the hurt of your childish touch, torn feathers
so easily loosened with love; if men
have confused you with a mere carnivore,
to the treacherous savant beneath fern,
(but, and strangely, never likened you more
to that cunning fish, Torpedo-Certain!),
it is possible that the mindful blind
did not discern the blossomed wings sprouting
from your shoulders, and that the mindful blind
did not interpret the omen glowing
in your forehead, the groove that I have scratched
there in blood, cross, chrism, enchantment, death,
a prayer meaning both perdition and salvation;
if they did not have the skill to reckon
you between a weasel or a woman,
then with whom can I share the revelation,
where shall I bury the gold I sweat out,
metalled in the coal-furnace of my heart,
when, turning from the high stairs, you depart?

Sonsong

after Koos Schuur

My father summoned me
for as much as a marble, a thruppence, a bird made of nothing

but of course I had to go along with that girl
climb up the roads and out of them
consider the flowers, observe the animals
and the lord in the heaven, the kingdom of heaven itself

My father summoned me
for as much as a farthing, as much as a slipper, as much as a wooden cigar

but of course I had to write down words again
that would endure after him, after me
and rhyme short lines for tales of horsemen
a fellow on a horse for my own sorrow

My father summoned me
for as much as a counsel, as much as a reason, as much as a worldly road

but of course I had to be elsewhere and elsewhere
all eyes and ears and my heart in my hand
a knight, a horseman, a world-disturber
who claimed he was building on reason and counsel

Autumnal Garden

after Dino Campana

To the spectral garden, to the voiceless
laurel with its green garlands,
to the autumnal dirt - a final farewell!
To the impenetrable, infertile terraces,
ruddy in the final sun, distant fertility
cries in a harsh cacophony:
it cries to the dying star
that has stained the marigold borders
with blood. Brass trumpets tear away
the vacuum of silence: the river sinks
into the sun-gilded sand: in the silence
glass statues stand, turned
on their heels at the entrance
and the exit of bridges:
all former states are gone.
From the distance like a choir, tender
and majestic, silence raises its breath
to my balcony: and in the odour
of laurel, in the bitter, failing stench
of laurel, from between the statues
immortal in the sunset, she appears
to me, transcendent, here.

Little Angel

little angel
your wings are made of iron
they can't sustain you
you fall to the ground
who can blame you, little angel

you rust away there
inside my ruined garden
tears destroy your face

let me be your burden
my little angel
oh my little angel

your wings are made of iron
you never paid
you never paid your rent
in heaven
my little angel
oh my little angel

my little angel
oh my little angel
live inside my basement
I'm much safer than the devil
my little angel
oh my little angel

I may be no good
but I'm not exactly evil
my little angel
oh my little angel

my little angel
oh my little angel
my little angel
oh my little angel

my little angel
oh my little angel
my little angel
oh my little angel

little angel, let me be your heaven
little angel, let me be your heaven
little angel, let me be your heaven
little angel, let me be your heaven
my little angel
oh my little angel
my little angel
oh my little angel
my little angel
oh my little angel
my little angel
oh my little angel

The Battlefield's Premonition

A blond-haired boy in a suit of red sewn
handkerchiefs stepped into sunlight and blazed
like a fire of burning silk. When he laughed
all the leaves spiralled down towards his crown
and the grass ran with the wind through the hills.
In his hand he had a salt-shaker which
he shook at the golden sparrows that twitched
amongst the fallen leaves. Grains of salt stilled
the snails in their quilts of mulch, shrivelling
them back to their ewers. Feathers of gold
floated free in the trembling air, foretold
that birds, even of gold and twittering
gaily without a care, should learn to dread
a blond-haired boy shaking salt, dressed in red.

Cat

My black coat is speckled with husks
of egg; fleas navigate the currents
of my fur, zig-zag over my itching skin;
ticks cluster behind my ears like jewels.
In the corner of each eye are crusted tears
of gunk. Infection has hitched cunningly
to my claws, my scratch will blacken
your blood in days. I'm no pussycat, I'm
just cat. I'm the shadow of the crossed path,
the ninth cat in a bad week, the cry like
a baby in the darkened hedge. I'm the mog
who shat the moon black. Don't tease my ear
with your finger, puss-puss me like some
stuffed toy. I'm the cat of black luck, the
hiss from the basement, the compiler of rats
at the back door, and nobody's purring pet.

Sandman

from worn rocks   and broken shells,
the friable   disintegrated bodies
of tiny crabs,   i became.
disparate grain   by disparate grain.

at the shore   someone
picked me up   in their cupped
hands   and poured me
into a crucible.   fire was passed
through me,   until i turned
into molten glass.   then i felt
her breath   blow me
into the shape   that filled her mind:
a bottle   resembling   a transparent
empty   man.

i wait.   to be filled.   to be darkened.
by her.

The Mermaid's Last Breath

The lens of the sky
a magnified beach:
clouds like ghosts of bones,
white delicate ribs;
shells of trilobites,
stippled skin of fish;
sea's discarded waste.

This is what she saw
as she floated face-up
in the breadth of a second
before she died.
Later, fishermen found her
thrown against the rocks,
her body a rotten carcass
of floating flesh.
They mistook her
for a mutilated seal,
and could not possibly have known
of her last moment's vision:
of a desolate non-water
beyond the trembling membrane
of life.

Seán Slammon

Seán Slammon found himself awake in sleep,
sucked up the black-furred chimney with the smoke.
Winged men had pulled his spirit through his ear
for no better purpose than a spiteful joke.
"We'll swap you with the body of a fox,
thus by daybreak you'll find yourself transferred."
So up a fox's rear they shoved poor Seán;
likewise the fox's soul was disinterred.
"Now you rest here amongst the bugs and lice,
while we take Fox to lie beside your wife.
We suggest you make the most of earth and grass,
for from this moment this will be your life."
But as the morning's light began to break
young Seán doubted he was indeed awake.

The Early Risers

Six hedgehogs the size of commercial vans
lay dozing on the lawn, their snouts blowing
six tempests of ripe breath at the washing.
The dew-sodden towels billowed on the lines
of the swivel-rail, turned like 'copter vanes
until the entire lawn and the creaking
garden shed, the six hedgehogs (still sleeping),
our neighbour's house, the hen house and the hens,
our house and the garden pond (with two bass)
rose up into the sky, dropping down worms,
clods of earth, sunken pennies, clothes-peg springs,
all kinds of stuff that had sunk through the grass,
and took us up above the highest storms,
the plum-purple sky, on rotating wings.

Medusa

your hair ties and unties itself as you sleep
eats mice that stray across your pillow

at daybreak you wander to the cliffs
look down into the thrashing sea

the floor of the ocean is full of the dead
turned to stone and sunken in their ships

your hair braids itself and caresses your breasts
your serpent's tongue parts your lips

evening comes and you lie on your bed
your hair is exhausted and falls asleep

The Archaeologist's Dream

In the ditch where I had fallen, beetles crashed
through grey leaves and brittle litter, worms raised
the soft lid of the soil, snails adjusted
their thick skirts, while toadstools secretly birthed
their offspring through trembling vents. All of time
was trapped in clay, where my mind moved
like a stone. I am the man of bones,
the echo of a man soaked into soil.
I am the ghost that haunts the worm-troubled earth.
The wet ditch is my mouth, and the moving creatures
are the language I invent. Their stumbling
becomes my stumbling vocabulary
towards an expression of self.
Listen for my voice, you who disturb my rest.

The Acorn Door

Beyond the acorn door I found

a blunted scissors   and a man with iron hair

seven goldfish   inside a glass cat

a woman of vinegar   pouring her heart out

a castle of cheese   turning green

a trumpet   that sucked in sound

a stammer's worth   of poetry

an exit sign   to the around-the-world-road

The Crankodile in the Black Nile

The river of oil takes the crankodile
in, seamlessly sealing itself once he's
down beneath its skin. His plated hull in
riveted squares, iron rusted inwards
to the joins, he eases himself through black
nothing. Nothing: what the river became
since the days of pyramids mushrooming
smoke rings as high as the moon; but the space
down here is his, truly empty of light.
This is what he was made for: the nothing;
the nothing-river thick with itself, thick
with airless suffocating bitumen.
The crankodile reaches the muddy floor,
thrashes down under silt, to nothing more.

Early One Summer

A man made of sunlight awoke on the edge
of the road. He was stretched for seven miles,
his mind at rest in a heap
of spaded earth. And he thought:
"I'll gather myself
and hold myself in
with a foxglove coat."
So he made for himself
a garment of foxglove bells,
each bell held
with a loop of grass.
And that's how he was
when we met,
his body a gathering
of startling blossom,
alive in the wetness of morning.

A Cloak of Owls

She wraps herself in a cloak of owls and enters the shaman's dream
and all the skies collapse inside the prophecies to come.
He watches moonlight dye her hair as she stands beside the stream;
she wraps herself in a cloak of owls and enters the shaman's dream.
Trumpets sound from mouths of birds, nothing is as it seems,
as time moves slowly backwards to creation's nascent Om.
She wraps herself in a cloak of owls and enters the shaman's dream
and all the skies collapse inside the prophecies to come.

Ghost

for Eileen Sheehan

Your father left his overcoat
when he departed that dark hill;
and though you seek to fill that space,
that space you cannot hope to fill.
Your father's fields are left untilled,
the creeping gorse will claim the land;
and even though you break the soil,
the hidden thorn will tear your hand.
Your father beckons from the earth,
his voice the music of a stream,
his body now a verdant growth
that encroaches pasture and dream:
"Do not be haunted by regret.
Live. You'll rejoin me sometime yet."

Waiting Patiently at the Stone Door

I have a letter in my pocket waiting to speak
and I need to hear the stone door turning

I rang the bell years and years ago
but the stone door opens slower than a year at a time

"open the stone door
the dogmen are barking

cars have left their shapes
where they rusted in the streets"

my voice evaporates without an echo
an impenetrable shadow mosses the door-face

I wait on the step catching light on my tongue
and all I can hear are the dogmen barking

the stone door is beginning its end
slower than a year at a time

I have a letter in my pocket waiting to speak

Comb

I broke a tooth on the tangled locks
of that dark-haired woman. My mouth was greased
with the grease from her un-sunned head. Only
the plughole of the bath holds more of her
than I. She keeps me on the shining lid
of the toilet cistern; lets me wait
until she's ready. No one is more loyal
than the one she drags backwards and forwards
through that hedge of hers. I live to be taken up
and put down. Waiting is my duty too. I
lie idle most of my days, hoping she'll
take me back near her bed. How I think
bitterly on the day I was replaced
by that silver lad. The one who spends
his days and nights a-straddle on her brush.

Grass

Along my flanks edges of me are cool
in the shadows of the trees. The rest of me
is out in the sun, brightly green. I'm green
everywhere, except when I'm not; but even in
the withering of me there's a memory
of green. My name is synonymous with green
and like that colour I'm innocence itself.
Everything comes to me for everything comes
to the floor, and I'm the floor of everywhere.
Even beneath the sea you'll find a version
of me. But most of the time you'll find me here,
wherever you happen to be. I'll be waiting. I remain
here for everyone. It is said I cover the dead, and actually
I do. But I much prefer the living. And the living I live
for most is my darling love. She steps barefoot onto me,
walks my length. I feel myself cooling under each step.
Then she undresses and begins to lie down.
First I feel the shadow of her shape, and then
her shape. I could grow into this. Usually I do.

Apple Pip

Into an apple I took a bite
apple pip, apple pip, apple pip
and there she was curled up tight
apple pip, apple pip, apple pip
a fine young woman with night-black hair
apple pip, apple pip, apple pip
what did she do to get in there?
apple pip, apple pip, apple pip
she ran around my fingers twice
apple pip, apple pip, apple pip
her skin was white and cold as ice
apple pip, apple pip, apple pip
I asked her would she be my bride
apple pip, apple pip, apple pip
but she brusquely pushed me to one side
apple pip, apple pip, apple pip
oh no dear sir, she said to me
apple pip, apple pip, apple pip
unless you retrieve from the cold dark sea
apple pip, apple pip, apple pip
these three things I tell you of
apple pip, apple pip, apple pip
and only then can I be your love
apple pip, apple pip, apple pip
first of all the salt in the sea
apple pip, apple pip, apple pip
every grain you must bring to me
apple pip, apple pip, apple pip
and when you have completed that task
apple pip, apple pip, apple pip

this is the next one I will ask
apple pip, apple pip, apple pip
bring me some water that isn't wet
apple pip, apple pip, apple pip
but you won't be quite finished yet
apple pip, apple pip, apple pip
between the water and the sand
apple pip, apple pip, apple pip
collect all the seashells in one hand
apple pip, apple pip, apple pip
when she had finished my apple was gone
apple pip, apple pip, apple pip
and then she vanished and so has my song
apple pip, apple pip, apple pip

Tao of Earthworm

Its ringed body foreskin after foreskin,
foreshortening itself through negative
ejaculation; sheathed in its own va-
cancy, disappearing its own full length;
casting aside wet vulval yawnings,
falls spent upon the lawn, limp; then, pulled
asunder by thrush, torn between blue tit,
blackbird, men fishing with poles; expectant
of the penile lips of trout, envy of
the minnow, anchored by a single prick.

On the Greymouse Bus

A mouse arrived at the mouse-stop

a grey mouse to Shadow Square

his tail was ringed in gold

a ring of gold the fare

I paid for a ride with my wedding ring

and stepped inside his ear

the hedges blurred like the sea in a shell

and life became a tear

None but the Invisible Nun

hiding under
a veil of sunlight
the invisible nun

stark naked before
his puzzled eminence
the invisible nun

thinner than
the eucharist
the invisible nun

a mist
passes the altar
the invisible nun

the priest
feels nothing
the invisible nun

her body
without stain
the invisible nun

the foolish novice
hides behind her
the invisible nun

unapparent on the head
of a pin
the invisible nun

you'll never know
when you see her
the invisible nun

Sister Nought
casts no shadow
the invisible nun

Crow

My black feathers offend daylight, my beak
offends everything else, tears up flesh, pulls
entrails from smashed bodies. And when I speak
that also is an offence, splintering
the air with obscene laughter. But night, night
is the time when I become night itself,
the squabbling chaos of my thoughts shouting
their own commands: to create a pure light
and begin the world again. God Myself
enters daylight, the first day of the weak
created for my mouth to snap and quell.
Everything that is, is my bloody work.
Yes, I am the black lice-ridden plumage,
am nature's nightmare of senseless damage.

The Enchanted Pond

Dressed in his leggings and shirt of mail,
and with a helmet of purest silver,
he dived into the sluggish waters of the enchanted pond.
And so dressed, in his leggings and shirt of mail,
and with a helmet of purest silver,
he pushed through the thick lips of the sea-hag's vulva,
where he was drawn inwards by the weight of his armour.
For a whole day he turned, in hopeless somersaults,
through the chaos of her womb. Until,
dressed in his leggings and shirt of mail,
and with a helmet of purest silver,
he birthed himself from his own dead mother.

Mother dead, own his from, himself birthed he
silver purest, of helmet a, with and
mail of shirt, and leggings his, in dressed until.
Womb her of, chaos, the through
somersaults, hopeless in, turned he
day whole, a for. Armour his, of weight the by
inwards drawn was he, where vulva hag's, sea the of
lips thick, the through, pushed he
silver purest, of helmet a, with and
mail of shirt, and leggings his, in dressed, so and.
Pond enchanted, the of waters, sluggish the, into dived he
silver purest, of helmet a, with and
mail of shirt, and leggings his, in dressed.

Bog Asphodel

Here I birth and here I am, tar water my start;
yet through the seeping space of bog
I erupt in yellow stars. Then nebulae
am I and I am a starnight of saffron.
Bog is the roof of the underworld,
where upside down the dead
walk with their feet shadowing the soles
of the living. Each step you take
you take onto the step of your dead self.
And down here I am the true night
of saffron stars. I am the Hades of
the dull and indifferent. Down you come,
down you come to my dunlit world,
where my roots bind the Heavens in place.
Cruppany I give to sheep who eat my flames
and down to Hades they crumble, boneless sheep
herding the souls of dullards. Pick me oh pretty
and pin me to your hair, and my saffron dust
shall bid you, shall bid you here.

All Things End, Well, End Well

hanging upside down the hanged man planted
his free foot in a cloud
and began to drag down the sky, saw it wobble
under the sun

his hair, truly free, brushed against the grass
and the grass
entwined itself in his head and he shook
his green meadow hair

and the houses slid to the sea and the city
hacked its thickened lungs
and the glistening blade of the sun severed
him free, truly free

Ode Nymph

Teenage thug, young dragonfly and damsel,
dressed in sloppy overcoat of pond,
known to give the lip to fat-head tadpole,
terror of slow rivers and beyond.
To earn a body made of vibrant metals
you'll peel your skin and leave it on a stalk,
and own the air with speeds transcending vision,
learn to dart above all human talk;
devour insects fresh from their own cradles;
sit still as death on fencepost and on stone.

Brain

If you were to pull me out I'd be very long.
I'm the second longest organ in the body,
but the other one is full of shit. I'm the one
though that carries all the woes, the one
expected to take the strain. The one everyone
refers to when they know nothing, and then
they blame me when I know less than them.
Sigmund Freud thought he knew all about me,
thought his thoughts were coming from me.
Personally, I think he was thinking through
his arse, but that's just me. He thought I had sex
on the boil. But I don't. I let that up to other
organs. Usually the smaller ones. The tongue,
perhaps. Or the wagging finger. Sex. It's
over-rated in my opinion. I rarely give it
a thought. Thinking about sex is a waste of time.
I've got better things to do. The other organs
depend on me. Especially the smaller ones.

On the Morning a President Ordered the Invasion of Iraq

Fascinated by the ants in the sugar-bowl first thing
in the morning, black-helmeted and moving about
as if pedalling on low and invisible bicycles,
he tried several experiments, starting with feeding them
to the goldfish; but found the goldfish disdainfully
disinterested. More fascinating was the fact that
the ants appeared unable to break the surface of the water
and paddled shallowly from one end of the fish-tank
to the other. Admiring of their perseverance he
rescued them one by one, gave them all a chance to dry out
on the window-sill with a heap of sugar to keep them
focussed. Then he tried to see how many he could keep
in a teaspoon without them crawling out, but found it almost
impossible to put them in there in the first place, for they could not be
forced to do anything against their will. All in all
he spent over an hour playing with the ants, found it difficult
in the finish to leave them and make his way to work. The last he
glimpsed of them was a swirling spiral of black dashes with legs
busying themselves around the tipped honey-jar he'd left
on the kitchen floor. He watched momentarily the viscous golden mess
spreading out along the tiles, then turned his back and made his way
towards the car and his dull job.

The Secrets of the Elephant

for Mark Liddy

we invented the elephant
so that with its wrinkled arse
we could leave an enormous enigmatic thumbprint
on your front lawn

we invented the elephant
so that mice could travel
through the tunnel of its nostril
on their holiday to the lung

we invented the elephant
so that beetles could carry
steaming suns of dung
into their dark larders of earth

we invented the elephant
so that we could open
the shells of peanuts
with the utmost extravagance

we invented the elephant
so that there would be some creature at least
who could remember
why we invented the elephant

He Dreams of His Ice-Lolly Castle

oh the child has licked his ice-lolly castle
and his tongue is yellow, yellow

and the king commands that the windows be closed
and the queen commands that the sky be shut down
and the tongue in the heavens is yellow, yellow
and the end of the world is a tongue

oh the child has licked his ice-lolly castle
and his tongue is yellow, yellow

the magician comes in his purple gown
and his hat is as pointed as the steeple in town
and the tongue in the heavens is yellow, yellow
and the end of the world is a tongue

oh the child has licked his ice-lolly castle
and his tongue is yellow, yellow

and mammy comes out with a broom and a shout
and she sweeps and she sweeps till the candles burn out
and the tongue in the heavens is yellow, yellow
and the end of the world is a tongue

oh the child has licked his ice-lolly castle
and his tongue is yellow, yellow

and the castle is gone, all melted away
and the king and the queen ruled for less than a day
and the tongue in the heavens is yellow, yellow
and the end of the world is a tongue

oh the child has licked his ice-lolly castle
and his tongue is yellow, yellow

and the boy throws the stick and it falls where it went
and the ants all swarm to a castle of scent
and the tongue in the heavens is yellow, yellow
and the end of the world is a tongue

oh the child has licked his ice-lolly castle
and his tongue is yellow, yellow

and the ants all yearn for a castle of ice
where the king speaks once and the queen speaks twice
and the tongue in the heavens is yellow, yellow
and the end of the world is a tongue

oh the child has licked his ice-lolly castle
and his tongue is yellow, yellow

The Existential Poet

his blue suit is made from the blue sea
it uncreases itself at the low tide
fills up at night with dark velvet folds
shines during the day
keeps secrets in its deep pockets

his poems are published on the moon
written with the footprints of astronauts
translated into many languages
all of which are silent
and communicable only through mime

jackdaws flying in tandem
with their own shadows
and stones at the bottom of a river
gazing up at their own reflections
are examples of his work

The City of Angels

As I strolled out in the City of Angels
as I strolled out in the city one day
I spied a young biker sprawled in the gutter,
dressed in black leathers, his skin pale as clay.

"I see by your chapter that you're Satan's Brother,"
he gurgled through blood as I passed by his way:
"Come sit down beside me, I'll tell who betrayed me,
I'm cut in the throat and I won't last the day.

I used to go riding with Death's Bloody Fathers,
I robbed and I pillaged and happy was I,
I cheated at cards and I stole from my mother
but that ends today for today I will die.

Get six other bikers and douse me with petrol
and don't steal my bike or I'll curse you to hell.
Burn me and the bike in this City of Angels;
if you do as I say you'll live your life well."

Then he gurgled his last and died in the gutter
and we doused him in petrol and watched his flesh burn
and we sold his good bike and divided the money
and spent it on women who had nothing to learn.

He'd forgotten to mention the one who betrayed him
but I knew who he was and made certain to tell
when I met the mad biker who'd cut his throat open
and we shared from the bottle and sang praises to Hell.

Ballad to My Invisible Mistress

As I idled in the whitethorn orchard,
waist-high in copper ferns,
a bird with a feathered crown of fire
sang from his palace of thorns

And moths rose up with their bodies of dust
confused by the burning sun,
shaken from the ferns as I passed by
thinking of my darling one

For I have a spiral of her hair
locked up in a secret book,
I've touched her heart beneath her skin
and drunk her thin white milk

Badger

As the moon tongues the earth with light
I snout the pebbled ground. Beetles
in their shining cassocks anoint
my razored teeth. Worms are bludgeoned
from my bludgeoning of soil. I
am the offspring of the moon, her
pathway of light the stripe of white
on my forehead, the blackened bulk
of my body the stale shadow
that enters the henhouse for blood.
I am the stench trailing the edge
of gardens, the householder's glimpse
of a god, the squat rummager
of rubbish.

Let's Drop a Box of Pins

Let's drop a box of pins on old Baghdad:
a pin is such a subtle kind of bomb.
We'll make the most of this game playing God.

From this far up the damage won't look bad;
in Texas they won't see each scarlet plume.
Let's drop a box of pins on old Baghdad.

A simple pin can pierce a tyrant's head;
bad luck if one should stray inside a womb.
We'll make the most of this game playing God.

SADDAM TAKES EVIL AXIS TO HIS BED.
UGH! HIM BIG BAD WICKED PETROLEUM.
Let's drop a box of pins on old Baghdad.

We dream of building ziggurats from blood;
let's do it far from Texas where there's room.
We'll make the most of this game playing God.

Children, mothers, fathers, those countless dead:
they'll cheer us as we justify their doom.
Let's drop a box of pins on old Baghdad:
we'll make the most of this game playing God.

A Pteranodon Reflects on Motherhood

From here, thick humid mist obscures the ground,
steaming up through the warm trembling air. But
her hollow reed-like bones vibrate with sound
she cannot hear. She turns, steers upwards, caught
by fear. She knows the cry that resonates
through her frame is the birthing call of *her*
whose hunger respects nothing, whose lust waits
for nothing; whose black thunderous heart will fear
nothing. She knows that eggs containing teeth
are slipping hot from the flexible slit
of a mother with neither love nor grief,
who will rear her children in blood and shit,
and teach them her creed of kill and despise,
the bones of the dead their nursery toys.

A House of Golden Thread

an angel lives on the tip of a pin in a house of golden thread
and his feet are cut to ribbons and flames pour out of his head
he pisses in a golden cup and calls it Babylon Wine
he's ragged, worthless, heaven-bereft, half-past turpentine

and Heaven's a piece of sewing that's falling loose at the seam
and Earth is another word for dirt, and Death is a word for dream
so fall asleep if you must, and fall asleep if you may
but shake your angel from his house and beg him, beg him to pray

for God has gone and left us, and driven off in a hearse
and the living are barely dead, and the dead are faring worse
and voices grow in our ears, like wiry downy hair
and Lucifer takes down the sun while standing on a chair

an angel lives on the tip of a pin in a house of golden thread
and his feet are cut to ribbons and flames pour out of his head
he pisses in a golden cup and calls it Babylon Wine
he's ragged, worthless, heaven-bereft, half-past turpentine

but what's the use of angels carousing in heaven drunk
their feathers mired, their hair aflame, their armour tarnished junk
so rouse yourselves from your pillows and call a maiden's name
and she'll come in from the sea-floor holding a glowing skein

with fish bones fine as needles she'll tightly sew your dreams
and seal those drunken fears in sleep, and fold them up in reams
and she'll take you to the region inside a curving shell
where Heaven is really Heaven and there's no such place as Hell

but an angel lives on the tip of a pin in a house of golden thread
and his feet are cut to ribbons and flames pour out of his head
he pisses in a golden cup and calls it Babylon Wine
he's ragged, worthless, heaven–bereft, half-past turpentine

The Way Back

That grey cat sleeps in the dusty spaces
of the moon's face. She never stirs a limb
while the moon's lit up, but only rises
on moonless nights. She is the starlight's whim
and may be glimpsed as troubled waves through grass
or the sheen of ice on a distant pond.
Holding your gaze, her eyes as bland as glass,
she'll mesmerize you till your heart's beyond
the threshold of the living. In the hedge
you'll awake, no thicker than a shadow.
You'll die this way nine times nine to the edge
of disappearance. The next thing you'll know
is you're a kitten. You'll climb the night's stairs
as high as you want, your fur bright as stars.

John W. Sexton was born in 1958 and is the author of four previous poetry collections: *The Prince's Brief Career*, Foreword by Nuala Ní Dhomhnaill, (Cairn Mountain Press, 1996), *Shadows Bloom / Scáthanna Faoi Bhláth*, a book of haiku with translations into Irish by Gabriel Rosenstock (Doghouse, 2004), *Vortex* (Doghouse, 2005), and *Petit Mal* (Revival Press 2009).

He also created and wrote *The Ivory Tower* for RTE Radio 1, which ran to over one hundred half-hour episodes. His novels based on this series, *The Johnny Coffin Diaries* and *Johnny Coffin School-Dazed* are both published by The O'Brien Press and have been translated into Italian and Serbian.

Under the ironic pseudonym of Sex W. Johnston he has recorded an album with legendary Stranglers frontman, Hugh Cornwell, entitled *Sons of Shiva*, which has been released on Track Records.

He is a past nominee for The Hennessy Literary Award and his poem *The Green Owl* won the Listowel Poetry Prize 2007. In 2007 he was awarded a Patrick and Katherine Kavanagh Fellowship in Poetry.